A LOOK AT U.S. ELECTIONS

HOW DOES VOTING WORK?

BY KATHRYN WESGATE

Gareth Stevens PUBLISHING

CRASHCOURSE

Please visit our website, www.garethstevens.com. For a free color catalog of all our high-quality books, call toll free 1-800-542-2595 or fax 1-877-542-2596.

Library of Congress Cataloging-in-Publication Data
Names: Wesgate, Kathryn, author.
Title: How does voting work? / Kathryn Wesgate.
Description: New York : Gareth Stevens Publishing, 2021. | Series: A look at U.S. elections | Includes bibliographical references and index. | Contents: Use your voice! -- Who can vote? -- Get registered! -- Where to vote -- Follow the rules -- Multiple methods -- Picking a party -- Choosing a candidate -- Counting the votes -- Get ready to vote!
Identifiers: LCCN 2019049339 | ISBN 9781538259603 (library binding) | ISBN 9781538259580 (paperback) | ISBN 9781538259597 (6 Pack) | ISBN 9781538259610 (ebook)
Subjects: LCSH: Voting--United States--Juvenile literature. | Elections--United States--Juvenile literature.
Classification: LCC JK1978 .W47 2020 | DDC 324.6/50973--dc23
LC record available at https://lccn.loc.gov/2019049339

First Edition

Published in 2021 by
Gareth Stevens Publishing
111 East 14th Street, Suite 349
New York, NY 10003

Editor: Kate Mikoley

Photo credits: Cover, pp. 1, 29 Hill Street Studios/Digital Vision/Getty Images; series art kzww/Shutterstock.com; series art (newspaper) MaryValery/Shutterstock.com; p. 5 PureRadiancePhoto/Shutterstock.com; p. 7 YinYang/E+/Getty Images; pp. 9, 13, 15, 17, 23 Hero Images/Getty Images; p. 11 Layland Masuda/Shutterstock.com; p. 19 Joseph Sohm/Shutterstock.com; p. 21 Burlingham/Shutterstock.com; p. 25 Diane Macdonald/Moment Mobile/Getty Images p. 27 Drop of Light/Shutterstock.com.

Printed in the United States of America

Some of the images in this book illustrate individuals who are models. The depictions do not imply actual situations or events.

CPSIA compliance information: Batch #CS20GS: For further information contact Gareth Stevens, New York, New York at 1-800-542-2595.

CONTENTS

Words in the glossary appear in **bold** type the first time they are used in the text.

USE YOUR VOICE!

You've probably voted before. It may have been for class president or where to eat dinner. U.S. government elections may be different than votes you've taken part in, but one thing is the same: Voting lets people have their voices heard.

Make the Grade

An election is an act of voting someone into a government position. Elections may work differently depending on who or what they're for.

WHO CAN VOTE?

To vote in a U.S. election, you must be a U.S. **citizen**. You must also be at least 18 years old by Election Day. In all states except North Dakota, you also need to be registered, or signed up officially, to vote.

Make the Grade

Some states have more rules about who can register. For example, some require that you've been a resident, or lived in that state, for a certain amount of time before Election Day.

GET REGISTERED!

You may be too young to vote now, but you can still learn how it works. Plus, some states let you register before 18. You won't be able to vote, but you can sign up so you'll be ready when your 18th birthday comes!

Make the Grade

Ask a trusted adult to help you look online and find out when your state lets you register to vote. It may be as young as 16 or 17!

Residents of Washington, D.C., and 38 states can register to vote online. In other states you need to fill out a form and mail it in. You can also register at your state or local election office and some other public offices. The website vote.gov has directions on how to register in each state or **territory**.

Make the Grade

People who live in most U.S. territories are U.S. citizens but can't vote in presidential elections. They can vote in local elections and elections that decide who will run for president.

Even if you're registered to vote, you need to make sure your **information** stays up to date. This means you need to change your registration information if you move. If you move to a new state, you'll need to register in that state.

Make the Grade

Some states take people who haven't voted in a while off their registration list. You should check your registration well before any election you want to vote in.

WHERE TO VOTE

Depending on where you live, you may need to be registered as early as a month before Election Day. Once you're registered, you'll need to know where to go to vote. The place you go to vote is called your polling place.

Make the Grade

If you live with an adult who votes, they probably know where their polling place is, but it can change! Voters should check their polling place before every election.

FOLLOW THE RULES

Rules for elections are often different from state to state. Some states require voters to show **identification** at their polling place. In other states, officials may double-check that your **signature** matches the one they have on file for you.

Make the Grade

Even among states that ask for identification the rules are different. Some require the identification has a photo, while others may accept a bill with your name on it as identification.

MULTIPLE METHODS

States choose how to record people's votes. Some states have voters fill in their answers on pieces of paper, called ballots. These may look sort of like a test where you fill in bubbles for your answers.

Make the Grade

In some states, voters use special machines. These may have buttons or touch screens and can record the votes right to a computer.

PICKING A PARTY

The most important, and often hardest, part of voting is choosing whom to vote for. In the United States, we have a two-party system. This means most voters choose **candidates** from one of two main **political parties**: Democratic or Republican.

Make the Grade

You can pick which party you want to belong to when you register to vote, but you don't have to. You may change which party you vote for throughout your life.

CHOOSING A CANDIDATE

Before joining a party or deciding to **support** any candidate, you should always do some research, or studying. The winner will make certain choices in office. You need to learn what the person stands for and if you agree with them on important subjects.

Make the Grade

A debate is when candidates answer questions and talk about changes they may make if elected. Watching a debate is a great way to learn if you agree with a candidate or not.

You can read up on candidates online or in a newspaper. Voter guides list candidates and say what they want to get done in office. They may also talk about past jobs they've had that have to do with the position they're running for.

Make the Grade

You can also find sample ballots. These show you what the real ballot might look like so you know what to expect when you get to your polling place.

COUNTING THE VOTES

How a winner is chosen depends on the election. Some elections are won through a popular vote. This is likely how you've voted on things before. Everyone's vote counts the same and the person with the most votes wins.

Make the Grade

Members of Congress, as well as leaders in many local and state positions, are elected through popular votes.

The popular vote doesn't decide the president or vice president. The Electoral College does. Each state has a number of electoral votes based on how many people live there. Electors from the party that wins the popular vote get to vote. Their votes decide the winning pair.

Make the Grade

The Electoral College was set up in the **U.S. Constitution**. It was seen as a **compromise** between having a popular vote or a vote in Congress to decide the president.

GET READY TO VOTE!

You may be too young to vote now, but you can prepare for when you're older and help others understand the importance of voting by doing the following:

- Ask adults in your life if they're registered to vote and if they plan to vote in the next election.
- Find out how old you have to be to register to vote where you live.
- Look at a sample ballot for the area you live in.
- Learn about the candidates running for election.
- Make a list of subjects you feel strongly about. See which candidates agree with you.

GLOSSARY

candidate: a person who is running for office

citizen: someone who lives in a country legally and has certain rights

compromise: a way of two sides reaching agreement in which each gives up something to end an argument

identification: a document that shows who a person is and has their name and other information on it

information: knowledge or facts about something

political party: a group of people with similar beliefs and ideas about government who work to have their members elected to government positions

signature: a person's name written in their own handwriting

support: to agree with and help someone

territory: a piece of land that is part of the United States but is not a state

U.S. Constitution: the piece of writing that states the laws of the United States

FOR MORE INFORMATION

BOOKS

Conley, Kate. *Voting and Elections*. Minneapolis, MN: Core Library, an imprint of ABDO Publishing, 2017.

Nelson, Kristen Rajczak. *How Do People Vote?* New York, NY: PowerKids Press, 2019.

WEBSITES

How Voting Works

www.ducksters.com/history/us_government_voting.php

Find out more about how voting works on this website.

Presidential Election Process

www.usa.gov/election

Watch a video and view an infographic to learn how the presidential election works.

Publisher's note to educators and parents: Our editors have carefully reviewed these websites to ensure that they are suitable for students. Many websites change frequently, however, and we cannot guarantee that a site's future contents will continue to meet our high standards of quality and educational value. Be advised that students should be closely supervised whenever they access the internet.

INDEX